MW01017060

Auckland Architecture

A Walking Guide

John Walsh

Photography: Patrick Reynolds

MASSEY
UNIVERSITY
PRESS

Handwritten inscription:

SLT RICHARD HORNE,

MID HAMISH HAHUNGA,

A GIFT TO THE WARDROOM

FOR THE FINAL WEEK OF OP PROJECTION
2019, FROM THE HOT BEACHES OF
HAWAII TO THE WELCOMING CALM OF
VICTORIA, US 4 KIWI JUNIOR OFFICERS
WERE HOSTED SPLENDIDLY FROM THE
OFFICERS OF OTTAWA.

AS A THANK YOU, TAKE THIS GUIDE
OF OUR HOME CITY FOR THE NAVY.
USE IT PERSONALLY OR FOR VLO
ACTIVITIES!

SAFETY BE ALWAYS WITH YOU

FAIR WINDS & FOLLOWING SEAS

AROHA - LOVE

THE KIWI JUNIOR OFFICERS

Contents

P.S. IF YOURE EVER IN TOWN IN A PROFFESIONAL OR PERSONAL CAPACITY, FEEL FREE TO GIVE ME A MESSAGE TO ASK WHATS HAPPENING AROUND THEN.

hamish.hahunga@nzdf.mil.nz

NGA MIHI, HAMISH

Introduction

The land now occupied by central Auckland has been inhabited since the fourteenth century, when Māori tribes settled the fertile isthmus they called Tāmaki, a place so naturally favoured it was also called Tāmaki-makau-rau (Tāmaki of a hundred lovers). Tāmaki seems to have been a flourishing, if occasionally contested, region by the mid-seventeenth century, 100 years before the English naval explorer James Cook navigated his way to New Zealand, and 200 years before the establishment of the colonial settlement of Auckland.

Auckland's official foundation may be ascribed to Governor William Hobson, who in 1841, the year after he had signed the Treaty of Waitangi with Māori chiefs, chose to make the place the capital of the colony of New Zealand, a status it lost in 1865. In the way of these things, the new capital was named for an imperial figure who had never been remotely near New Zealand; in this case Lord Auckland, the contemporary Governor-General of India, whose career was about to be blighted by the disastrous British retreat from Kabul in the First Afghan War.

Immigrant ships quickly began to arrive, and a rough and ready settlement coalesced around Commercial Bay, at the bottom of what is now Queen Street, before spreading up the Parnell ridge to the east and the Ponsonby ridge to the west, and south up the

Queen Street gully to Karangahape Road. This catchment, which incorporates the modern Auckland CBD and parts of its central-city suburbia, is the focus of this book. Despite Auckland's often careless approach to its built heritage, this area contains more than 150 years' worth of architectural history. From the street, you can read the story of Auckland's progress, its filling in and its going up, and the architectural evolution that accompanied the city's economic development.

The buildings of a city, whether civic or commercial, residential or religious, express the values, ambitions and aesthetic inclinations of the people who, at a particular moment in time, commissioned their design and construction. Architecture is a good guide to the zeitgeist. Accordingly, central Auckland is a pattern book of the styles that have commanded architectural allegiance over a century and a half: the various Revivalisms — Classical, Gothic and Baroque — that were fashionable in Victorian and Edwardian Britain and exported to Britain's empire; the turn-of-the-century Chicago School that is synonymous with confident American capitalism; soft-core inter-war Modernism in its Stripped Classical and Art Deco guises; International Modernism, house style of the post-war corporation; and current expressive form-making, enabled by computer-aided design and composite material technology.

A city's buildings are also a testament, and a measure, of its architectural talent. Able architects have designed impressive buildings in Auckland. In the nineteenth century most of the city's architects were immigrants, men — the word is used advisedly, given the historically gendered nature of the architectural profession — who often came from modest backgrounds in Scotland or Ireland. In their social circumstances, the pupillage nature of their training and their command of the practical details of construction, Auckland's early architects were not so far removed from the master masons who had shaped European cities for a thousand years. As architecture became more professional, and the city grew, local practices were established; many had their hey-day and then declined, or morphed into new firms. The fortunate few are remembered in their surviving buildings. As well as providing a guide to Auckland's more interesting buildings, this book acknowledges the architects who designed them.

It is organised into half a dozen walks (with public transport close at hand) around the city and its waterfront, and takes in significant streets such as Karangahape Road and Ponsonby Road, important civic buildings such as the War Memorial Museum and the Art Gallery, and popular urban spaces such as the Domain and Wynyard Quarter. Some of the buildings are monumental, some are modest, and all have a story to tell: a city is the sum of its disparate parts.

A note about access & classifications

This book is intended as a footpath guide to the architecture of central Auckland, but many of the featured buildings and structures are open to closer inspection, at least to some extent. The Auckland War Memorial Museum and Auckland Art Gallery of course welcome visitors, as does the publicly funded Artspace. Holy Trinity Cathedral is open to the public, as are St Patrick's Cathedral and All Saints Church. The Leys Institute is a public library, and the glasshouses in the Wintergardens are open every day of the week.

Ellen Melville Hall may be appreciated from adjacent Freyberg Place, and Old Government House from the University of Auckland gardens, which also afford good views of the Maclaurin Chapel. The scene on North Wharf can be observed from the restaurants that front onto the public walkway by the harbour edge, and some of the silos in Silo Park are carved open at ground level. An internal public laneway passes through the Imperial Buildings, connecting Queen Street and Fort Lane. Cafés in the Synagogue and Community Centre, and in St Kevin's Arcade, present leisurely opportunities to experience those buildings.

Smith and Caughey's is a functioning department store, the Civic Theatre is open for performances only, and the Sky Tower can be accessed for a price. (A head for heights is a pre-requisite.) Grafton Bridge and the Lightpath are always open for pedestrians.

Many of the buildings in this guide are listed as Historic Places (Category 1 or 2). These appellations are applied by Heritage New Zealand, a government agency that identifies New Zealand's significant and valued historical and cultural heritage places. Category 1 historic places are of special or outstanding historical or cultural significance or value; Category 2 historic places are of historical or cultural significance or value. It should be noted that listing does not necessarily entail protection.

BRITOMART & THE WATERFRONT

A HUB FOR ALL RECRUITS GRANTED THIER FIRST EVER SHORE LEAVE...
— HAMISH

Auckland started out as a port, and the area around the docks was for decades the most vital part of town. For much of the twentieth century, though, the city's waterfront was out of bounds to the public. That's changed now, and the centre of gravity of the CBD is shifting back to the water's edge. This route takes in two urban-revival precincts: Britomart and Wynyard Quarter.

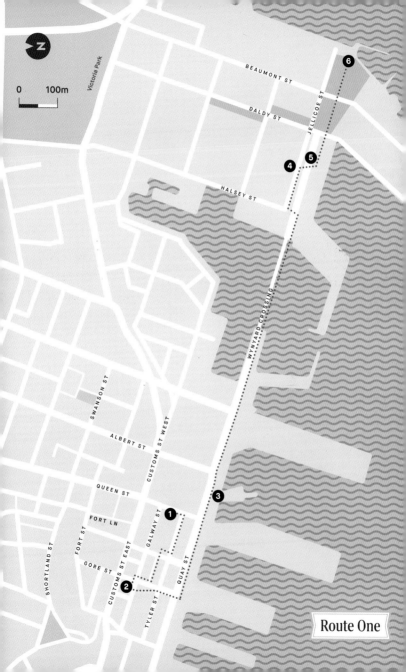

Route One

Chief Post Office

12 Queen Street
John Campbell, 1912
Historic Place Category 1

John Campbell (1857–1942) loved Edwardian
Baroque architecture, and he was ideally placed to
implement his preference as a national style. The
Scot was in charge of the design of New Zealand
government buildings for more than 30 years, nearly
half of them (1909–1922) spent as the country's first
Government Architect. In this nation-building phase
of New Zealand's history post offices were essential
public amenities — a remote country's portals to
the world — and their importance was expressed in
their architecture. Made of white Ōamaru stone and
Coromandel granite, Campbell's Chief Post Office
features a Baroque panoply (London's 1910 General
Post Office was an acknowledged influence): arches
and cartouches, half-columns with Ionic capitals,
a pediment and a parapet and, most flamboyantly,
cupolas at either end of the building. In the early
2000s, the Chief Post Office was converted, by Mario
Madayag, Jasmax and Salmond Reed Architects, into
Britomart Railway Station.

Australis House & A. H. Nathan Warehouse

37 Galway Street
Mitchell & Watt (Australis House); A. P. Wilson
(A. H. Nathan Warehouse); both 1904
Historic Place Category 1 — Australis House
Historic Place Category 2 — A. H. Nathan Warehouse

Australis House (formerly the Entrican Building) and the A. H. Nathan Warehouse and Condiments Factory were built on reclaimed land near Auckland's shipping wharves as premises for prosperous colonial importing companies. In the 1990s, a public campaign saved the buildings, and their Victorian and Edwardian neighbours, from ill-considered redevelopment. Restored as one project in 2016 by architects Peddle Thorp, the two buildings are now an integral element of the Britomart heritage precinct. Both buildings face two ways: south to Customs Street, and north (shown here) to the new Takutai Square. Architect A. P. Wilson (1851–1937) topped the Customs Street façade of the A. H. Nathan Warehouse Factory with Romanesque arches; the north side of the building has a plainer neo-Classical façade. Australis House, designed by the practice of John Mitchell (c1859–1947) and Robert Watt (1860–1907), features Baroque detailing on the south face; elegant *sgraffito* (plaster tracery) has been applied by Peddle Thorp to the originally unadorned north façade.

Ferry Building

"YOU WILL NEVER FIND A MORE
WRETCHED HIVE OF SCUM AND
VILLAINY"
    — HAMISH

99 Quay Street
Alexander Wiseman, 1912
Historic Place Category 1

Throughout the twentieth century harbour boards, unsurprisingly in a maritime trading nation, were powerful political entities in New Zealand's port cities, and they proclaimed their importance in their architecture. The Ferry Building, commissioned by the Auckland Harbour Board, occupies an absolutely central waterside site — it is still the downtown ferry hub — at the foot of the city's main street and across the road from the former Chief Post Office (now Britomart Railway Station). The building was designed by Alexander Wiseman (1865–1915), who may have been inspired by a famous precedent in another Pacific port, the Beaux-Arts-style Ferry Building (1898) on San Francisco's Embarcadero, designed by A. Page Brown (1859–1896). Auckland's Ferry Building is designed in the Imperial (or Edwardian or English) Baroque style. Corinthian columns, entablature and gabled pediments in Sydney sandstone leap up and out above a Coromandel granite foundation. The clock tower once housed a time ball; a fifth storey was squeezed into the building in the 1980s.

ASB North Wharf

12 Jellicoe Street
BVN Donovan Hill and Jasmax, 2013

ASB North Wharf, which anchors the eastern end of
a long street that terminates in Silo Park to the west,
was the first new big building in the Wynyard Quarter
precinct. The flash north façade perhaps provides a
clue to the building's provenance: it was designed by an
Australian-led architecture partnership (BVN Donovan
Hill, from *there*, in association with Jasmax, from *here*) for
an Australian-owned bank (ASB). The colours of a sun-
kissed land are deployed in the interests of corporate
identity — yellow being a client brand colour — and also
as a gesture towards indigeneity. Fins on the east end
of the building allude to the bark of the pōhutukawa,
while the shimmering screen on the western block was
generated from an artist's image of the dead leaves of
native trees. Framed cut-outs disrupt the wall of 'leaves'
— the screen admits light into and allows views out of
the building's interior — and mark the building as the
product of its moment. On the east block, a funnel topped
by what looks like a giant Ottoman turban is an integral
component of the building's natural ventilation system.

North Wharf

Wynyard Quarter
Fearon Hay Architects, Architectus,
Wraight + Associates and Taylor Cullity Lethlean, 2012

Auckland city started out by the harbour, grew up next
to the quays, and then turned its back on the waterfront
for a century. The public knew when it was not wanted:
an iron fence marked off the domain of the Harbour
Board and maritime businesses. Things changed in the
late 1990s when the Viaduct Basin became the home
for yachting syndicates contesting the 2000 America's
Cup. This in turn became the catalyst for dockside
development, which has reached west, following a
masterplan by Architectus, into a former industrial area
now called Wynyard Quarter. The first stage of this new
precinct of offices and apartments was North Wharf,
a scheme devised by Wraight + Associates and Taylor
Cullity Lethlean that incorporates a heritage cluster of
old concrete silos. Fishing boats still berth alongside
a waterfront promenade that is flanked by a restaurant
row — a refurbished wharf shed and two complementary
structures — designed by Fearon Hay Architects.

Silo Park

Beaumont and Jellicoe Streets
Taylor Cullity Lethlean and Wraight + Associates, 2011

Over the past 20 years, maritime cities all around the world have rediscovered their waterfronts, and old working — or not working — ports have been redefined as real estate. In Auckland the repurposing of the waterfront as a site for hospitality venues, corporate offices and upmarket apartments began when the Viaduct Harbour was redeveloped for the America's Cup regatta held in 2000. Development now focuses on Wynyard Quarter. Two key issues attend maritime renewal projects such as Wynyard Quarter: the provision of public access and the treatment of legacy infrastructure that gives urban waterfronts their gritty character. At the western edge of Wynyard Quarter, Silo Park, designed by Taylor Cullity Lethlean and Wraight + Associates, both provides popular amenity and preserves historical character. The centrepiece is a cluster of 1960s concrete silos built to store cement; themselves sculptural objects in the landscape, the structures are now used as art and exhibition spaces.

EAST SIDE

The lower east side of Queen Street is part Establishment, part Bohemia. Law firms and insurance companies have long colonised Shortland Street; shops and cafés occupy the cluster of small streets near High Street. Auckland Art Gallery is not far away, sited on a corner of Albert Park. On the other side of the 1880s park, old merchant houses face across Princes Street to the campus of the University of Auckland.

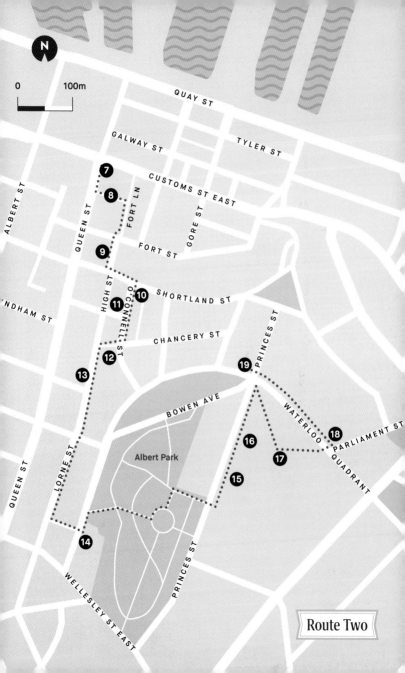

N

0 100m

QUAY ST

GALWAY ST

TYLER ST

ALBERT ST

QUEEN ST

CUSTOMS ST EAST

FORT LN

GORE ST

(7)

(8)

FORT ST

(9)

HIGH ST

O'CONNELL ST

SHORTLAND ST

(10)

(11)

NDHAM ST

CHANCERY ST

(12)

PRINCES ST

(13)

(19)

BOWEN AVE

WATERLOO QUADRANT

(18)

PARLIAMENT ST

LORNE ST

Albert Park

(16)

(17)

QUEEN ST

(15)

(14)

PRINCES ST

WELLESLEY ST EAST

Route Two

Dilworth Building

Corner of Queen Street and Customs Street East
Gummer & Ford, 1927
Historic Place Category 1

The Dilworth Building sits on the best corner of
Auckland's busiest downtown intersection. Throughout
the day, its Portland stone façades, looking north and
west, glow in the sunlight that struggles to reach into
the Queen Street cavern. Commissioned to provide
rental income for a school for disadvantaged boys,
the building was designed by William Henry Gummer
(1884–1966), an outstanding figure in New Zealand's
architectural history. Before the First World War Gummer
worked in London for Sir Edwin Lutyens (1869–1944)
and in Chicago for Daniel Burnham (1846–1912), and on
the Dilworth Building he dipped deeply into the Beaux-
Arts box of tricks, deploying pilasters and entablature,
consoles and spandrels, mouldings and motifs. The
building could have been even better: it was meant to
have a twin, also with a corner softened by a concave
curve, on the opposite side of the street. The proposed
composition — 'Urbis Porta' — would have provided a
graceful gateway to Auckland's main shopping street.

Imperial Buildings

44–48 Queen Street and 7 Fort Lane
Edward Mahoney & Sons, 1886–1911
Historic Place Category 2

The Imperial Buildings are a warren of Victorian
and Edwardian structures between Queen Street
and Fort Lane, which in 2012 were revived and
re-ordered around an internal public walkway by
Fearon Hay Architects. The building fronting Queen
Street was designed by Thomas Mahoney (c1854–
1923), son of the significant colonial architect and
Irish immigrant Edward Mahoney (c1824–1895). Two
cinemas operated in the premises in the first half of
the twentieth century — Everyman's Picture Theatre
(1915, architect Hugh Grierson) and Roxy Theatre
(1935, architect George Tole). The restoration of
the Imperial Buildings — the complex now houses
offices and restaurants — is a landmark project in
a city that has been careless with its built heritage.
It is also associated with a new civic approach to
public space. Coincident with the restoration, Fort
Lane, on the Imperial Buildings' east side, has been
transformed from a dingy and dangerous alley into a
Melbourne-style laneway of cafés and restaurants.

Jean Batten Place
Departmental Building

7 Fort Street, 9 Jean Batten Place
and 12 Shortland Street
John Thomas Mair, 1942
Historic Place Category 1

The building named for pioneer aviator Jean Batten (1909–1982), holder of many long-distance solo flight records, was an early commission of the progressive Labour government elected in 1936. Government Architect John Thomas Mair (1876–1959) took the hint and forswore neo-Classical references, opting instead for a restrained Moderne style. Construction of the building, which had three street façades, was a highly visible process, if not as audible as it might have been; unusually, the steel frame was welded, not rivetted, to reduce construction noise. After war service as a United States military headquarters, the building reverted to government use until it was sold off in the deregulation binge of the late 1980s. After a decade as a backpackers' hostel and following a heritage row, the Category 1 building was gutted and its exterior preserved as the lower-level face of a new office tower. Across Shortland Street, Grierson, Aimer & Draffin's Chicago-style South British Insurance Building (1929) has so far escaped a similar fate.

General Buildings

Corner of Shortland and O'Connell Streets
Bloomfield & Hunt, 1928 (extended 1977)
Historic Place Category 1

Throughout the twentieth century Shortland Street
was a preferred location for the chambers of
professional gentlemen, one of whom was William
Read Bloomfield (1885–1969), whose architecture
office was in Yorkshire House (now the General
Buildings), which he designed in the boom years
before the Great Depression. Bloomfield was probably
the first Māori qualified architect — his mother was of
Ngāti Kahungunu descent. He attended the University
of Pennsylvania and his familiarity with the restrained
ornamentation of the Chicago School is evident in
the General Buildings. But Bloomfield could turn his
hand to any style — Art Deco, Spanish Mission and
Arts and Crafts in the 1920s and 1930s; International
Modernism in the late 1940s and 1950s. His other great
passion was aviation. A fighter pilot in the First World
War, he was shot down over France and captured
by the Germans; in the Second World War he was in
charge of training New Zealand air force cadets.

Alliance Assurance Company Building (Administrator House)

5 O'Connell Street
Rough and Hooper, 1925

The architecture of banking and insurance companies is the architecture of confidence, these days expressed as flamboyant, self-conscious contemporaneity. But a hundred years ago, solidity and permanence were the qualities advertised by masonry buildings featuring pedestals, pediments and Classical columns. Clad in Ōamaru limestone on a base of Nelson marble, the Alliance Assurance Company Building (now Administrator House) is typical of the early twentieth-century money temples. Its designer, Basil Hooper (1876–1960), was an able Arts and Crafts architect. Born into a missionary family in India, Hooper grew up in the Waikato and started his architecture career in then-wealthy Dunedin before studying and practising in London. Back in Dunedin, he designed many accomplished houses before moving to Auckland in the early 1920s. 'There was always beauty and motif in his work,' a biographer wrote, and Hooper, one suspects, would approve of the current dignity of O'Connell Street, lately remade as a 'shared space' free of parked cars.

Pioneer Women's & Ellen Melville Hall

Corner of High Street and Freyberg Place
Tibor Donner (Auckland City Council), 1962

Modernism in Auckland owes much to a generation of Middle European architects — more in sync with Le Corbusier (1887–1965) and Ludwig Mies van der Rohe (1886–1969) than Anglocentric locals — who practised in the city through the middle of the twentieth century. Tibor Donner (1907–1993) was one of these Modernist émigrés. Born in a region of the Austro-Hungarian Empire that is now in Serbia, Donner came to New Zealand with his family when he was 20 and excelled as a student at the University of Auckland's School of Architecture. In 1946 he started a 20-year career as City Architect, designing many civic buildings, including the hall named for the prominent feminist politician and lawyer Ellen Melville (1882–1946). With its legible structure of pilotis, beams and columns, butterfly roof and cantilever, and its material palette of concrete, steel and glass, the building is expressly Modernist. In 2017 it was sympathetically refurbished by Stevens Lawson Architects.

Canterbury Arcade

47 High Street
Peter Beaven, 1967
Historic Place Category 2

Peter Beaven (1925–2012) was one of the most
compelling figures in the last half-century of New Zealand
architecture. He was a great admirer of the neo-Gothic
architectural tradition of his native Christchurch and
an outspoken, although nuanced, critic of Modernism,
which he considered impersonal and anti-humanist. His
romanticism is evident in Canterbury Arcade, perhaps his
only significant Auckland commission. The arcade cleverly
connects a pair of 1914 buildings on Queen Street with a
narrow frontage on High Street. This High Street façade
is the best architectural surprise in downtown Auckland:
a slim slice of Paris inserted into an eclectic row of early
mainly twentieth-century mid-rise buildings. Shutters and
balconies give depth to the façade, and the progressively
diminishing height of the five above-ground floors, with
their floor-to-ceiling windows, enhances the building's
vertical proportions. There's even a garret on the top,
although it probably doesn't come with a starving artist.

Auckland Art Gallery
Toi o Tāmaki

Corner of Wellesley Street East and Kitchener Street
Grainger & D'Ebro, 1887/FJMT and Archimedia, 2011
Historic Place Category 1

Unlike Auckland's museum, serene on its elevated parkland plinth, the city's art gallery receives no favours from its location. After winning the competition to design the building, Melbourne architects John Grainger (1854–1917) — father of the famous pianist and composer Percy Grainger — and Charles D'Ebro (1850–1920) had to deal with an awkward site on a downhill corner of Albert Park. The architects gave the building the full French Château treatment: pediments, pilasters and mansard roofs. There's a lot going on, but the cleverest element might be the curved vertical section, topped by a Moorish tower, that allows the building to turn the 120-degree corner. In 2011, a complex restoration and extension project was completed; the star of this show is the soaring kauri roof canopy that hovers above the new forecourt and North Atrium. The design architect was again an Australian — Richard Francis-Jones of Sydney firm FJMT, who worked alongside local practices Archimedia and conservation specialists Salmond Reed Architects.

Old Arts Building
University of Auckland

22 Princes Street
Roy Lippincott and Edward Billson, 1926
Historic Place Category 1

It's hard to believe now, but the much-loved Old Arts
Building at the University of Auckland — at its centre
a clock tower decorated with a filigree of native flora
and fauna — was very controversial when it was
completed. Outraged locals variously described the
building, which is made of concrete faced with luminous
Mount Somers stone, as 'freak architecture', 'Maori
Gothic', 'unBritish', and a 'wedding cake'. Much of the
criticism was motivated by chauvinism. The competition
to design the building had been won by American
architect Roy Lippincott (1885–1969) and Australian
draughtsman Edward Billson (1892–1986). Both had
been working in Australia for another American, Walter
Burley Griffin (1876–1937), the architect of Canberra.
(Lippincott married Griffin's sister Genevieve.)
Lippincott has an intriguing place in New Zealand
architecture; he was an innovative ornamentalist
with, as one critic puts it, both historicist and proto-
Modernist tendencies. He designed many institutional
and commercial buildings and houses in Auckland
before leaving New Zealand in 1939 for California,
where he practised until his retirement in 1958.

Maclaurin Chapel

18 Princes Street
Gummer, Ford, Hoadley, Budge and Gummer, 1964

In a neighbourhood busy with buildings of historical
heft, the Maclaurin Chapel is a moment of repose: its
good manners preclude overt religiosity, hence its
ecumenical appeal. The hexagonal chapel and adjoining
rectangular hall sit on an edge of the university's
grounds, once the gardens for the Old Government
House (overleaf). On its street side, the building recedes
to allow for a small forecourt; on its other, it surmounts a
sloping lawn. Morning and afternoon light streams into
the chapel through strongly vertical sections of glazing.
The chapel commemorates Fleet Air Arm pilot Richard
Maclaurin Goodfellow, who was killed in 1944, and his
uncle, Richard Cockburn Maclaurin, a distinguished
mathematician. It was designed by the firm of Gummer,
Ford, Hoadley, Budge and Gummer, a successor to the
practice founded by William Henry Gummer (1884–1966)
and Charles Reginald Ford (1880–1972) in the Beaux-
Arts 1920s — John Gummer was William Gummer's
son — and is consistent with what has been called
the 'moderate Modernism' of later Gummer & Ford.

Old Government House

Princes Street and Waterloo Quadrant
William Mason, 1856
Historic Place Category 1

Government House — or 'Old Government House' —
dates from Auckland's time as the capital of New
Zealand (1841–1865), and was built as a residence
for the governor of the colony. The design of the
country's first 'Great House' was an early victory for
Italy over Britain in what architectural historian John
Stacpoole called New Zealand's 'battle of the styles'
between Classicism and English Gothic. Proponents
of the latter style were offended by the 'dishonest'
presence on a timber building of stonework details
such as quoins, corbels and keystones. Government
House was a viceregal residence until 1969, when
it was taken over by the University of Auckland. (The
grounds are open to the public.) The building was
designed by William Mason (1810–1897), architect
to the Auckland Provincial Council. In the early
1860s, the years of the Otago gold rush, Mason
followed the money to Dunedin, where he set up a
practice with Nathaniel Wales (1832–1903), which
survives as New Zealand's oldest architecture firm.

Courtville

9 Parliament Street
A. Sinclair O'Connor, 1919
Historic Place Category 1

Just over the road from the university, and a short walk
from downtown offices and shops, Courtville has long
been a desired residence for freer spirits who prefer
city life to have some urbanity. The dozen-unit building,
also known as Corner Courtville, is one of four surviving
apartment buildings on Parliament Street designed by
architect Arthur Sinclair O'Connor (1884–1943), who came
to New Zealand from Australia before the First World War
and went on to become an apartment specialist during
Auckland's inter-war period of inner-city growth. (The
post-Second World War flight to suburbia put the brakes
on that for decades.) Constructed of reinforced concrete
and brick — and possessing the city's first residential
elevator — Courtville is distinguished by a façade that
contrasts projecting bay windows with receding balconies,
all topped by a domed lantern above a splayed entrance
at the street corner. A public campaign and intervention
from then-Conservation Minister Helen Clark saved the
building from destruction in the demolition-happy 1980s.

Northern Club

19 Princes Street
James Wrigley and Edward Rumsey, 1860s
Historic Place Category 1

Among the British institutions transplanted to Victorian New Zealand was the gentleman's club. Versions of this home-away-from-home for moneyed males popped up in all of the colony's main cities, and rather belatedly in Auckland, which was always less proper than the planned settlements to the south. The Northern Club was established in 1869, and in the same year the club bought the Royal Hotel, an Italianate brick building constructed only two years earlier to a design by architect James Wrigley (c1837–1882). The building was then reconfigured to house the club by another architect, Edward Rumsey (1824–1909), a pupil of the famous English Gothic Revivalist Sir George Gilbert Scott (1811–1878), who was lured for a while from Australia by the wealth of gold-rush Dunedin. The most dramatic of the Northern Club's various alterations is the resolutely contemporary Wintergarden addition (2008) designed by Fearon Hay Architects. Since 1927, Virginia creeper has grown on the two street façades of the original building.

WEST SIDE & MID-TOWN

Queen Street is the main drag of Auckland —
and perhaps the nation. The street follows
the course of the Waihorotiu Stream, which
is still there, under the asphalt. Over the
years, as development spread up the gully,
Queen Street progressively accumulated
commercial and institutional buildings
designed in the architectural styles of their
time. West of Queen Street, the Catholic
Cathedral is out-spired by the Sky Tower,
proclaiming the presence of the casino.

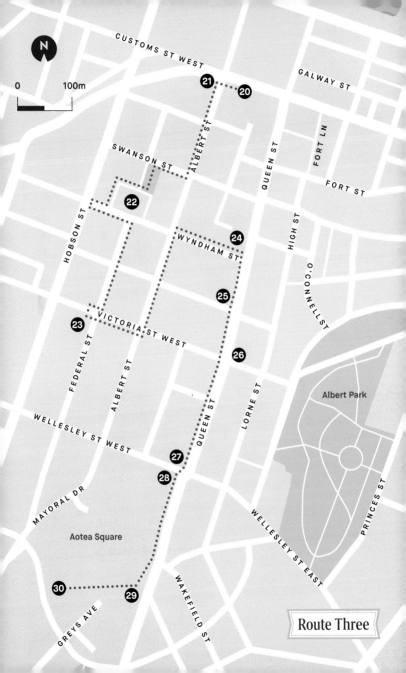

N

0   100m

CUSTOMS ST WEST

GALWAY ST

㉑ ㉚

SWANSON ST

ALBERT ST

QUEEN ST

FORT LN

FORT ST

㉒

WYNDHAM ST

㉔

HOBSON ST

HIGH ST

O'CONNELL ST

㉕

㉓

VICTORIA ST WEST

㉖

FEDERAL ST

ALBERT ST

QUEEN ST

LORNE ST

Albert Park

WELLESLEY ST WEST

㉗

㉘

MAYORAL DR

Aotea Square

WELLESLEY ST EAST

PRINCES ST

㉚

㉙

GREYS AVE

WAKEFIELD ST

Route Three

Customhouse

20

**22 Customs Street, corner of Customs
Street West and Albert Street
Edward Mahoney & Sons, 1888
Historic Place Category 1**

In nineteenth-century New Zealand, architecture
provided evidence of colonial advancement, and
Auckland's civic boosters must have swollen with pride
at the sight of the new Customhouse, completed just a
year after the Art Gallery, and in the same grand French
Renaissance style. How far the city had come since
its makeshift beginnings a few decades earlier. The
career of the building's architect, Thomas Mahoney
(c1854–1923), followed a similar trajectory. Mahoney
arrived in Auckland as an infant with his Irish parents.
He joined his father's architecture practice in 1876,
and with him designed numerous banks and hotels,
and Catholic schools and churches. Mahoney won the
government competition for the Customhouse after
a trip to London, where he was evidently inspired by
the Marshall & Snelgrove department store on Oxford
Street. Public agitation saved the Customhouse from
demolition in the 1970s and, in a nice historical irony,
the restored building now serves as a duty-free store.

West Plaza

21

1–3 Albert Street
Price Adams Dodd, 1974

More than 40 years after its construction, West Plaza
is still the most elegant modern building in downtown
Auckland; its presence among the ubiquitous,
easily partitioned boxes favoured by developers and
corporate tenants seems miraculous. The building
concept was produced by Neville Price, an architect
of flair and entrepreneurial inclination who later
spent many years practising in California before
returning to Auckland. The precedent often cited for
West Plaza — although not by Price — is the famous
Pirelli Tower (1958) in Milan, a 32-storey skyscraper
designed by Gio Ponti (1891–1979) and Pier Luigi
Nervi (1891–1979). However, 18-storey West Plaza is
a sleeker building, elliptical in plan where the Pirelli
Tower is tapered and, thanks to the close columns of
louvres on the north side, even slimmer in appearance.
Things are a bit convoluted nearer ground level, but
the eye doesn't linger there; instead, it takes in the
bespoke grace of West Plaza's pinstriped façade.

Cathedral of St Patrick & St Joseph

22

43 Wyndham Street
Edward Mahoney and Thomas Mahoney, 1884–1907
Historic Place Category 1

The ground occupied by St Patrick's Cathedral, as it is commonly known, is the epicentre of Catholicism in New Zealand. It was there, early in European settlement, that an Irish congregation led by a French bishop made its stand among Protestant British colonists. Jean Baptiste Pompallier was granted the Cathedral site in 1841 and built a timber church that was replaced in 1848 by one made of scoria. Construction of a new masonry cathedral designed by Irish immigrant Edward Mahoney (c1824–1895) began in the 1880s with the nave and tower; stage two — including the sanctuary, sacristy, high altar, side chapels and baptistery — was completed in 1907, probably under the direction of Edward Mahoney's son Thomas. The Mahoneys employed the Gothic Revival style, evident in the cathedral's steeply-pitched slate roof, external buttressing, lancet windows and broached spire. Not coincidentally, perhaps — commissioning bishop John Luck was a friend of the family of prominent English Gothic Revivalist architect, and Catholic convert, Augustus Pugin (1812–1852). Restoration and interior additions were undertaken by Salmond Reed Architects and Warren and Mahoney in 2005–2007, and St Patrick's Square was then successfully reworked by Boffa Miskell.

Sky Tower

23

Corner of Victoria Street West and Federal Street
Craig Craig Moller, 1997

The 328-metre Sky Tower is such a ubiquitous
presence on the Auckland skyline that it's both easy
to ignore and hard to miss. Whatever one thinks of the
tower — and it has been controversial — it certainly
performs valuable service as a compass needle for
directionally challenged drivers lost in the amorphous
tracts of Auckland suburbia. The observation and
telecommunications tower is a tour-de-force of
reinforced concrete construction, designed by architect
Gordon Moller and engineer Beca Group to withstand
200-kilometre-per-hour winds and a magnitude 8
earthquake. The tower's 12-metre-wide shaft, which
contains three elevators and a stairwell, is supported
by eight 'legs' based on foundation piles drilled
12 metres into sandstone. The bulb at the top of the
shaft, beneath the telecommunications mast, houses
restaurant and observation floors, and a bungee-
jump platform. Sky Tower is a built advertisement for,
and constituent part of, the SkyCity complex, which
occupies much of three city blocks and includes a
casino (if the tower is guilty, it's by this association),
conference centre, theatre, hotels, restaurants and bars.

151 Queen Street

24

151 Queen Street
Dino Burattini with Peddle Thorp & Aitken, 1988

In the mid-1980s the state relaxed its grip on New
Zealand's economy and the country developed
a sudden crush on capitalism. Among the agile
operators who seized the opportunities presented
by market deregulation were merchant bankers
Michael Fay and his business partner (and exemplary
case of nominative determinism) David Richwhite.
Their company commissioned Sydney architect Dino
Burattini (1933–2000) to design an office tower in
mid-downtown Auckland. Unhampered by committees
or cautious shareholders, Fay and Richwhite pursued
their vision for a signature building with unusual
singlemindedness and a generous budget. The cladding
of bronze reflective glass gives an expensive gleam to
the building, which is articulated as three slim towers,
a graceful effect achieved by projecting building-
high bays of mullion-less windows. At ground level the
building confronts the familiar Auckland handicap of a
sloping urban topography; the large-scale atrium offers
some redress. Local architect Brian Aitken mastered
the technical challenges of a then advanced building,
which has retained its design and material quality.

Landmark House

25

187–189 Queen Street
Wade & Bartley, 1930
Historic Place Category 1

The building now known as Landmark House was
commissioned by the Auckland Electric Power Board,
the public body in charge of the city's electricity supply
for most of the twentieth century. The board, which was
abolished in the 1990s, was proud of its buildings. Its
civic sensibility is evident in the 1940s sub-stations
— Stripped Classical with a touch of Art Deco — that
still dot Auckland's suburbs and, especially, its ornate
and stylistically eclectic Queen Street headquarters.
Architects Norman Wade (1879–1954) and Alva Bartley
(1891–1979), partners in a busy Auckland inter-war
practice, designed the eight-storey building to look
tall; when completed, it was described as a 'miniature
skyscraper'. On its moulded concrete façade narrow,
mullioned windows and a corner tower topped with a
turret achieve a vertical effect. The building opened on
the same day as New Zealand's first hydro-electric dam.

AMP Building

Corner of Queen Street and Victoria Street East
Thorpe, Cutter, Pickmere & Douglas, 1962

In the early 1960s, the AMP Building announced the
arrival in Auckland — a little belatedly and in a rather
truncated form — of the heroic International Style. The
building's glass curtain walls and clean lines injected
sudden glamour into a main street dominated by
low-rise Victorian and Edwardian masonry buildings.
The AMP Building was a clear homage to Skidmore,
Owings & Merrill's Lever House (1952) on New York's
Park Avenue — the seminal tower that, along with
Ludwig Mies van der Rohe's (1886–1969) nearby
Seagram Building (1958), was to set the direction of
international corporate architecture for two decades.
'Every architect working on office buildings at that
time was in love with glassboxes,' said the AMP
Building's designer Jack Manning, of the practice
Thorpe, Cutter, Pickmere & Douglas. 'Less is more' was
the Modernist mantra, but in this case, more may have
been better. The 11-storey AMP Building deserved to
be taller, but, with its slim, stainless-steel mullions,
green spandrel panels and opaque, tinted windows,
it is still elegant half a century after its construction.

ROUTE THREE | 65

Smith & Caughey Building

27

Corner of Queen Street and Wellesley Street West
Roy Lippincott, 1927
Historic Place Category 1

In 1880 Marianne Smith opened a drapery shop,
and was soon joined in the business by her brother
Andrew Caughey. This was the beginnings of Smith &
Caughey's, now Auckland's sole-surviving family-owned
department store. The design of the Smith & Caughey
Building testifies to the familiarity of its American-born
and -trained architect Roy Lippincott (1885–1969) with
the work of Chicago School architects, including the
famous high-rise pioneer Louis Sullivan (1856–1924).
Smith & Caughey's has a formal resemblance to the
larger-scaled Carson, Pirie, Scott and Company Store
(1904) that Sullivan designed for a prominent corner
site in downtown Chicago. The massing of the Smith
& Caughey Building is Sullivan-esque, as is the use
of large arched windows, cast-iron reliefs and other
decorative façade elements. (Both Sullivan and
Lippincott would have been puzzled by the dictum
of Viennese Modernist Adolf Loos that ornament is
crime.) Before the 1966 addition of a top floor, the
pilasters that stretched up the façade reached above
the parapet, emphasising the building's verticality.

Civic Theatre

267 Queen Street
Bohringer, Taylor & Johnson, 1929
Historic Place Category 1

28

Entrepreneur Thomas O'Brien developed a chain of cinemas around New Zealand in the 1920s. Evidently, he had the gift of the gab: at the end of the decade he persuaded a bank to lend him — unwisely for it, happily for Auckland — the huge sum of £180,000 to build the country's biggest picture theatre on a prominent Queen Street corner. In this golden age of film — the talkies were the latest thing — the escapism of the movies was complemented by the fantasy settings of the new 'atmospheric' picture palaces. O'Brien engaged Melbourne cinema specialists Bohringer, Taylor & Johnson to design the Civic Theatre, and young project architect Thomas Leighton (1905–1990) was despatched to Auckland, along with scenic artist Arnold Zimmerman (1897–1985). The Beaux-Arts-trained Zimmermann, who later worked on Sydney's Luna Park and Anzac Memorial, did not hold back on the Civic. Exterior motifs on the Art Deco building include sunbursts, scrolls and dancing maidens; the interior is a concoction of Moorish walled gardens, Persian minarets and plaster-cast Buddhas and elephants, topped off, above the 2700-seat main auditorium, by a rendering of the night sky, twinkling with stars.

Town Hall

29

301–317 Queen Street
J. J. and E. J. Clark, 1911
Historic Place Category 1

Like all local authorities in colonial New Zealand,
Auckland City Council oscillated between pride and
parsimony. In 1880 the council selected a site for a
town hall; 25 years later it advertised a competition for
the building's design. The winner was the Melbourne
practice of John James Clark (1838–1915), a prolific
designer of numerous significant civic buildings in
Australia, and his son Edward James Clark (1868–1951).
On Auckland Town Hall, the Clarks deployed the Baroque
Revival style that was the default architectural setting
of the British Empire in its pomp. Gravitas is conveyed
by a façade of Ōamaru limestone and base of Melbourne
bluestone. London's Lambeth Town Hall (1908) is
cited as an influence, but the building also has some
similarity with Fremantle Town Hall (1887) in Western
Australia, designed by the rival Melbourne practice
Grainger & D'Ebro, architects of Auckland Art Gallery
(1887). All three buildings respond to the problem of an
awkward triangular site with a clock tower positioned
at the confluence of the neighbouring streets.

City Council Administration Building

30

1 Greys Avenue
Tibor Donner (Auckland City Council), 1966

Every city has a Modernist building that architects like and most other people don't. Auckland's polarising exemplar of mid-century Modernism is the City Council Administration Building, designed by Tibor Donner (1907–1993), City Architect from 1946 to 1967. For architects the building's clarity, scale and composition — steel for the skeleton and aluminium frames and glass spandrels for the curtain wall — are design virtues, but from a populist perspective the building is too big and too boring. 'A stack of egg crates' was one contemporary verdict. Some projects just go on for too long: Donner started to design the Civic Administration Building in the early 1950s, but it wasn't completed until 1966. By then, International Modernism was losing its momentum. Another handicap: the building is isolated on a corner of a large square; being too undefined and too porous, the square has never really worked as a public plaza. The building has good bones, though, and may have a second act as an apartment complex.

GREYS AVENUE & K'ROAD

Greys Avenue is a street of diverting
buildings that runs from mid-town
up to characterful Karangahape
(K') Road. Over their history, both
streets have fluctuated between
rise and fall but have retained their
particular characters. More sustained
development, centred on a commuter
rail station, means that affluence
will soon impinge on diversity.

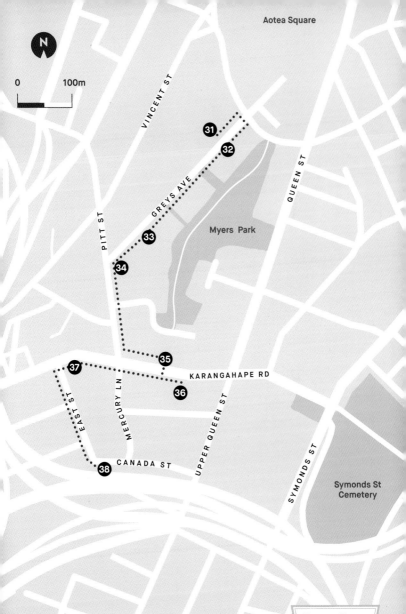

Aotea Square

N

0   100m

VINCENT ST

31
32

GREYS AVE

PITT ST

Myers Park

QUEEN ST

34

33

35

36

KARANGAHAPE RD

37

EAST ST

MERCURY LN

UPPER QUEEN ST

CANADA ST

38

SYMONDS ST

Symonds St
Cemetery

Route Four

Lower Greys Avenue Flats

95–113 Greys Avenue
Gordon Wilson (Housing Division, Ministry of Works), 1947
Historic Place Category 2

Greys Avenue is a graceful city street thanks to its plane trees, planted with great foresight by the council in 1871, and also to some of its buildings. Its most urbane architecture is a group of four Modernist, medium-rise concrete apartment blocks that step up the slope, hard up against the footpath. Commissioned by the government in the wake of local slum clearance, the 50-unit public housing project was directed by the architect in charge of state housing design, Gordon Wilson (1900–1959). Wilson's purposeful career is synonymous with New Zealand Modernism, and with the social housing programme of the First Labour Government (1935–1949). In 1936 Wilson was appointed Chief Architect of the new Department of Housing Construction (later the Housing Division of the Ministry of Works) and in that capacity, at a time of Anglocentric chauvinism, he employed talented European émigrés such as the Viennese architects Ernst Plischke (1903–1992) and Frederick Newman (1900–1964). Wilson served as Government Architect from 1952 until his death seven years later.

Parklane

32

68 Greys Avenue
Wade & Bartley, c1922

Parklane is a handsome apartment building in a city
that's still getting used to apartment living. It sits
four-square on its street and steps down into Myers
Park, offering its fortunate residents a rare prospect
of urban greenery. But it's the building's biography
that is of greater significance. Parklane was originally
the Auckland factory of the company founded in
Dunedin in 1862 by Scottish immigrants John Ross
and Robert Glendining. By the end of the nineteenth
century, when Dunedin was New Zealand's wealthiest
city, Ross and Glendining's eponymous enterprise
employed thousands of people in its local woollen mill
and clothes-making factories and warehouses around
New Zealand, and on the company farms that supplied
them. The company was a paternalistic employer, and
its Auckland factory, which was designed by Norman
Wade (1879–1954) and Alva Bartley (1891–1979) and
opened in the early 1920s, was welcomed as a provider
of decent female jobs in a notoriously rough part of
town. In the early 1990s, after the factory had closed,
the building was converted into an apartment block,
with three added floors, by architect Richard Priest.

Synagogue & Community Centre

33

108–116 Greys Avenue
John Goldwater, 1967

John Goldwater's Synagogue and Community Centre has the calm and assured presence of a fully resolved building. It does so many things so well: it provides an attractive edge to the street; it meets the topographical challenges of a site that ascends Greys Avenue at the front and drops into Myers Park at the rear; it offers privacy and protection to a community that has reason to be vigilant; and it makes excellent use of a central courtyard as both an organising principle and a sheltered plaza perfectly suited to Auckland's humid climate and blustery weather. Goldwater (1930–2000) was the architect son of an architect father and an admired teacher at the University of Auckland's School of Architecture. The influence of the great Finnish architect Alvar Aalto (1898–1976) has been discerned in the Synagogue and Community Centre, in particular Aalto's Säynätsalo Town Hall (1952), another clearly expressed, multi-functional brick courtyard building. The architecture and material composition of the Synagogue and Community Centre can be experienced in the street-level kosher café.

Central Fire Station

34

40 Pitt Street
D. B. Patterson, Lewis and Sutcliffe, 1944

The Central Fire Station is a survivor of an era in
which institutional buildings, through their design and
materials, suggested permanence. In the case of fire
stations, especially, this made psychological sense —
you want to think that an emergency service will always
be there for you — even if Classical proportions and
masonry heft did not necessarily equate to seismic
strength. (In contrast, contemporary fire stations, as
lightweight and flexible as big family houses, privilege
function and code-satisfying performance over
aesthetic messaging.) Sited on a commanding height
by a busy intersection, the Central Fire Station is one
of Auckland's most prominent Art Deco buildings. In
the period between the wars, New Zealand's architects
helped themselves to a smorgasbord of styles, and
Daniel Boys Patterson (1880–1962), architect of
the Central Fire Station, was at least as stylistically
promiscuous as his peers. Classical, Georgian Revival,
Gothic Revival, Moderne — Patterson essayed them all,
on banks and churches, cinemas and schools, hospitals
and houses, over the course of a long and prolific career.

St Kevin's Arcade

35

183 Karangahape Road
William Arthur Cumming, 1924

For nearly a century, the fortunes of St Kevin's Arcade
have followed those of Karangahape (K') Road. Between
the wars, the street was a vibrant middle- and working-
class retail strip, but in the 1960s it started to fall on
hard times as tens of thousands of residents of adjacent
inner-city suburbs were displaced by motorway
development. Anchor department stores eventually
closed and the sex trade moved in: the area was not
exactly family-friendly. But economic decline had its
up-side: many Victorian and Edwardian buildings have
survived, as have many small, idiosyncratic shops,
some of them housed in K' Road's most interesting
building, St Kevin's Arcade. The arcade, which connects
K' Road with Myers Park, was designed by William Arthur
Cumming (1860–1947), who at the time employed in
his office the extraordinary Esther James (1900–1990)
— model, adventurer, entrepreneur, designer and
builder. The light-filled café at the north end of the
arcade offers a glimpse of Myers Park, set out in 1915
by landscape gardener Thomas Pearson (1857–1930);
nowadays the park is best avoided at night. St Kevin's
Arcade was restored by Glamuzina Architects in 2016.

Artspace

36

300 Karangahape Road
Mark Brown Fairhead & Sang, 1973

Much of the attention paid to post-war Modernism
in Auckland has focused on The Group, a loose
collective of University of Auckland graduates who
self-consciously set out to establish a New Zealand
architecture. Light and airy, with simple materials,
exposed structural elements and modest budgets,
houses designed by The Group were ostentatiously
unostentatious, even a bit raw. But not all Auckland
architects were committed to a regionalist or
nationalist agenda. Peter Mark Brown (1929–1978)
and Alan Fairhead (1926–2010), for example, looked
to International Modernists like Richard Neutra
(1892–1970) in California and Harry Seidler (1923–
2006) in Sydney for inspiration, and their practice
pursued a sleeker, more glamorous Modernism in the
1950s and 1960s. In the early 1970s, by then joined
by Ron Sang, they designed the Newton Post Office
on Karangahape Road. The building featured a bas-
relief (extant) by artist Guy Ngan. In the 1990s, part
of the building was converted by architect Nicholas
Stevens into the publicly supported contemporary
gallery Artspace. Recently, architecture practice
Bureaux further reconfigured the gallery.

Ironbank

37

150–154 Karangahape Road
RTA Studio, 2009

When completed in 2009, Ironbank was the first significant new piece of architecture to appear on K' Road in a generation, and it prefigured the street's gradual but accelerating revival. Designed by RTA Studio, an innovative practice founded in 1999 by Richard Naish and Tim Melville, Ironbank is a complex building that addresses the very different conditions of the streets that bound it. On its north side, the building's low profile and glass-fibre reinforced-concrete façade defers to its Victorian and Edwardian K' Road neighbours, but on its southern side (shown here) the building rises dramatically above workaday Cross Street, presenting itself as three six-storey towers of steel-clad boxes. The stacking is askew and looks a little precarious — if those were containers down at the port you'd suspect a crane operator had been working under the influence. Ironbank is a particularly expressive example of the often striking architecture commissioned by its owner, a family-owned landlord company with a periodic inclination to embark on a (well-costed) design adventure.

Nelson Street Cycleway

38

From Upper Queen Street to Victoria Street West
Monk Mackenzie Architects and LandLAB, 2015

The Nelson Street Cycleway — or Lightpath: Te Ara i Whiti — is one of numerous projects around the world inspired by the 2009 High Line project in New York, in which an elevated section of a redundant Manhattan railway line was turned into a linear park. (The High Line was itself prefigured in 1993 by the similar Promenade Plantée in Paris.) In Auckland's case, an obsolete motorway offramp was repurposed as a cycleway and pedestrian path by architects Hamish Monk and Dean Mackenzie, and landscaper Henry Crothers. With its bright pink surface and highly visible night lighting, the Lightpath is both amenity and advertisement. It offers extended and unexpected views of the cityscape and harbour and provides some respite from the car traffic that suffocates Auckland, and also promotes the cause of a cyclable and walkable city. The Lightpath is integrated — notionally, if not altogether convincingly — in Auckland's growing cycle network. For pedestrians it is best accessed via the new Canada Street bridge, at the foot of Mercury Lane on the south side of Karangahape Road.

TO PARNELL

At the east end of K' Road the graceful Grafton Bridge leads to the gracious Domain, Auckland's oldest park. It's impossible to imagine the city without the Domain, and hard to imagine the contemporary provision of such generous public space. Two of Auckland's best-loved buildings — the Museum and Wintergardens — occupy privileged places in the Domain; beyond the Museum, and almost as well-sited, are the various components of Holy Trinity Cathedral.

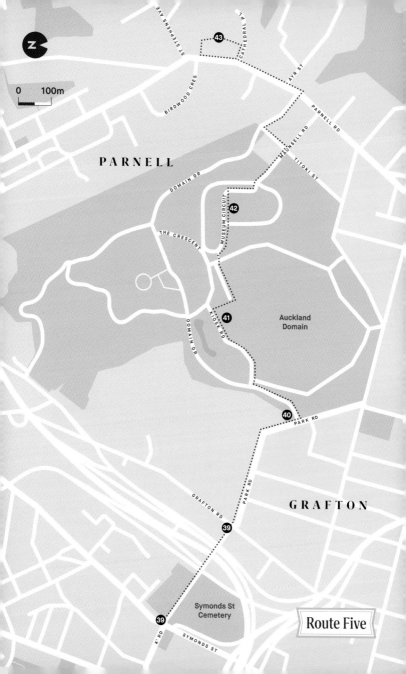

Route Five

Grafton Bridge

39

Linking Symonds Street and Karangahape Road with
Grafton Road and Park Road
Robert Forbes Moore and Karl (Charles) Rosegger, 1910
Historic Place Category 1

Grafton Bridge, which replaced a rickety footbridge over
the gully separating the city from Auckland Hospital
and the Domain, was a heroic enterprise for a young city
and a triumph of contemporary concrete engineering.
Nearly 300 metres long, the bridge is supported by
a 97-metre load-bearing central arch — the 'false
piers' at either end primarily serve an aesthetic
purpose — which, at the time of construction, was
the world's largest single span of reinforced concrete.
The bridge was technologically and commercially
challenging; its builder, the Ferro-Concrete Company
of Australasia, was bankrupted by the job, which had
to be completed by council staff. The chief engineer
was Royal Engineers veteran Robert Forbes Moore
(c1865–1938), but it seems design credit should have
been shared with Karl (Charles) Rosegger (1877–1919),
a young American-trained Central European engineer
whose backstory included arrest by Tsarist police in
Poland, political exile in Siberia, and escape via the
Gobi Desert, China, Tibet and French Indo-China.
Grafton Bridge was strengthened early this century
and, after an ill-fated experiment with their removal,
suicide prevention screens were re-installed.

Domain Gates & Statues

40

Park Road and Domain Drive
Gummer & Ford with Richard Oliver Gross, 1936

In the early 1930s, local businessman William Elliot,
who had partially funded the Domain Wintergardens,
paid for an ornamental gateway on the park's western
boundary. Elliot, as patron, picked the project's
architect: William Henry Gummer (1884–1966), of the
practice Gummer & Ford. In turn, Gummer engaged
sculptor Richard Oliver Gross (1882–1964), a memorial
specialist who had carved the frieze on the façade
of the War Memorial Museum. Gummer's gateway,
made of soft volcanic stone — Putaruru vitric tuff,
also known as Darley Dale sandstone — is centred on
two asymmetric plinths, each supporting a sculpture
by Gross. One, unobjectionably, is the stone figure
of a swan; the other, on the larger plinth, is a more-
than-full-size bronze statue of a naked male athlete,
a discus thrower or shot putter. The nude in classical,
heroic pose was an aesthetic trope of the times —
Gross's athlete is a less fetishised version of the
bodies beautiful in *Olympia,* Leni Riefenstahl's film of
the 1936 'Nazi' Olympiad — but in Auckland it excited
instant controversy. For a decade, moral campaigners
tried to have the statue removed or 'modified'.

Wintergardens &
Temperate &
Tropical Houses

41

Auckland Domain
W. H. Gummer and Charles Reginald Ford, 1921 and 1928
Historic Place Category 1

In 1843 Governor Fitzroy made the wisest political
decision in Auckland's history when he set aside
200 acres as the public reserve that became the
Domain. That was a lot of land for a cash-strapped
colonial city to maintain, and apart from some playing
fields the Domain remained untamed through the
nineteenth century. (In 1899 a newspaper reported
that blackmailers were preying on couples pursuing
'immoral intentions' in the park.) Respectability was
promoted by the successful Industrial, Agricultural and
Mining Exhibition in the Domain in 1913–1914. William
Henry Gummer (1884–1966) was then commissioned
to design the Wintergardens. The result suggests the
influence of his former employer, the great British
architect Sir Edwin Lutyens (1869–1944), and Lutyens'
frequent collaborator, the eminent garden designer
Gertrude Jekyll (1843–1932). A pair of barrel-vaulted,
steel-framed glasshouses frame the Wintergardens'
enclosed courtyard. One, the Temperate or Cool
House, is full of exotic flowering plants; the other, the
Tropical or Hot House, designed when Gummer was
in practice with Charles Reginald Ford (1880–1972),
barely contains some dramatic equatorial species.

Auckland War Memorial Museum Tāmaki Paenga Hira

Auckland Domain
Grierson, Aimer & Draffin, 1929
Historic Place Category 1

42

A BUILDING TO GET LOST IN
THOUGHT FOR HALF A DAY IF
YOU WANTED.

WIDE RANGING IN INFORMATION
OPEN BY DAY, BUT BREATHTAKING
TO VIEW AT NIGHT, BATHED IN
COLOURED LIGHT. — HAMISH

Auckland's museum sits serenely on the edge of
a dormant volcanic cone that was once a site so
contested by Māori tribes that it bore the name
Pukekawa, the hill of bitter tears. A portico of Doric
columns on the building's north face declares
allegiance to the Parthenon — if you're going to
reference Classical architecture, why not evoke
the seminal work in the Western canon? — and,
like the Parthenon, the museum is a votive temple
erected by a grateful community. (The reconciliation
of the building's dual purpose as war memorial
and museum has often been challenging.) The
museum is the product of a 1922 international
design competition won by local architects, and
war veterans, Hugh Grierson (1886–1953), Kenneth
Aimer (1891–1960) and Keith Draffin (1890–1964).
Above a Coromandel granite base, the building
is clad in imported Portland stone. (Concrete
was used for the 1960 rear addition.) A frieze of
battle scenes is inscribed in the stone, as are
the names of First World War battles — a place-
name poem of New Zealand service and loss:
Lone Pine, Armentières, Bellevue Spur, Polygon
Wood, Crevecoeur, Jericho and Jordan Valley. An
extension by architect Noel Lane, featuring a large
copper and glass dome, was completed in 2006.

Holy Trinity Cathedral

43

Parnell Road and St Stephens Avenue
Benjamin Mountfort/Charles Towle/Richard Toy/
John Sinclair/Fearon Hay Architects, 1898–2016
Historic Place Category 1 — St Mary's Church

Medieval cathedrals were hugely expensive and took ages to build, but as far as their design went it didn't really matter; in architecture and religion, nothing much changed over the centuries. But protraction became a problem once aesthetic evolution and liturgical innovation raced ahead of cathedral construction capacity. Design disjointedness became almost inevitable. Auckland's Anglican cathedral, developed over 120 years, is a clear case in point. The oldest element is St Mary's (opposite), a Gothic Revival timber church designed by Benjamin Mountfort (1825–1898). Completed in 1898, St Mary's served as the cathedral until 1973. A new brick cathedral was designed in 1940 by Charles Towle (1896–1960), but was not realised for half a century; by the early 1970s, only the chancel had been built. Richard Toy (1911–1995) picked up the project and designed the nave (page 104), which was completed in 1992. By then, St Mary's had been moved from its site across the road and placed alongside the cathedral's west face. A visitor centre designed by John Sinclair was added north of the nave in the 1990s, and in 2016, on the south side of the cathedral, Fearon Hay Architects' Bishop Selwyn Chapel (page 105) opened to widespread acclaim.

TO PONSONBY

Walk west along K' Road and you come to Ponsonby Road, a street that's just as interesting, if a little less intense. If any Auckland street has a sunny disposition, it's Ponsonby Road: it's flat, it runs along a ridge, and its buildings have a human scale. Ponsonby is old, for Auckland, and its main street retains a core of Victorian and Edwardian buildings. The more successful modern interventions have been stitched into this existing fabric.

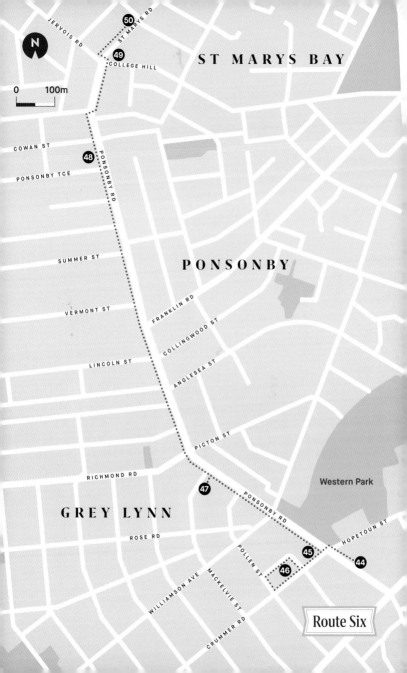

N

JERVOIS RD

ST MARYS RD

50

49
COLLEGE HILL

ST MARYS BAY

0   100m

COWAN ST

48

PONSONBY TCE

PONSONBY RD

SUMMER ST

PONSONBY

VERMONT ST

FRANKLIN RD

COLLINGWOOD ST

LINCOLN ST

ANGLESEA ST

PICTON ST

RICHMOND RD

Western Park

47

PONSONBY RD

GREY LYNN

ROSE RD

HOPETOUN ST

POLLEN ST

45

44

WILLIAMSON AVE

MACKELVIE ST

46

CRUMMER RD

Route Six

Newton Police Station & Barracks

1 Ponsonby Road
John Campbell, 1906
Historic Place Category 2

John Campbell (1857–1942) certainly knew how to make institutional buildings look institutional. After his arrival in New Zealand in 1882 the Glasgow-trained architect spent 40 years working for the government. In that period he designed post offices, courthouses, gaols, lunatic asylums and, at the apogee of his career, Parliament Buildings in Wellington. (In familiar New Zealand fashion, only the first stage of this project was completed.) Campbell also included police stations in his repertoire. The Newton Police Station and Barracks was built at a time when the inner-city working-class suburbs of Ponsonby, Newton and Freemans Bay posed various behavioural challenges — social, political and criminal — to established order. The building has some resemblance to the architect's much larger Dunedin Prison (1898). Both exhibit the Queen Anne Revival trait of exposed brick courses relieved by masonry bands and window surrounds picked out in a contrasting colour. The resulting effect, at Newton Police Station, is a building that's trussed as tight as a suspect under arrest. The building is currently used as a community art venue.

Allendale

45

50 Ponsonby Road
Architect unknown, 1893
Historic Place Category 1

George Allen was a saddler who did very well in
colonial Auckland. By the early 1890s he could afford
a corner lot on the Ponsonby ridge, recently made
more desirable by the introduction of horse-drawn
trams that travelled along Ponsonby Road to and from
the city. Allen commissioned — from an unknown
architect or perhaps a builder — a substantial Italianate
villa, a gracious house featuring deep verandahs with
ornate wrought-ironwork on the street frontages
of both floors. (There are few better responses to
Auckland's close climate and changeable weather
than an upper-level verandah.) The house is topped
by a turret — a feature of many contemporary grand
houses in the neighbourhood — which overlooks
Western Park, the public reserve that opened a few
years before Allendale was built. Allendale's fortunes
mirror the colourful history of a now-gentrified part
of town. In the century after its construction it served
as a boarding house, doctor's rooms, private hospital,
hostel for alcoholics and upmarket restaurant. In 2013,
Salmond Reed Architects restored the building and
completed a modern addition for the charitable trust
that has owned and occupied Allendale since 1989.

Vinegar Lane

Between Pollen Street and Crummer Road
Isthmus, 2011

46

The city block behind Allendale is the site of what its master-planner Isthmus — an urban design and landscape architecture company — describes as 'Kiwi urbanism'. Culturally tempered intensification might be another way to put it: Vinegar Lane is an attempt to find a compromise between the familiar standalone housing of Auckland suburbia and the large apartment block that has few popular precedents in the city. Vinegar Lane is an urban subdivision comprising around 30 six-metre-wide freehold lots on which four-storey, built-to-the-boundary terrace houses are progressively being constructed to designs by different architects. Small-scale businesses may occupy the ground-floor level of the buildings, in keeping with the mixed-use character of the neighbourhood. The project is a fortuitous outcome of the 2008 Global Financial Crisis, which killed off a planned commercial development that disregarded the local building scale. 'Vinegar Lane' alludes to the history of the site, which was occupied by a yeast factory that was a pungent presence in this part of Ponsonby from 1910 until the end of the twentieth century.

Mackelvie Street Precinct

Ponsonby Road and Mackelvie Street
RTA Studio, 2012

47

The Mackelvie Street Precinct is an adept
exercise in placemaking that, through the
creation of laneways and small courtyards,
knits together small, seismically-strengthened
buildings on Ponsonby Road and a row of
new sympathetically-scaled shops and
commercial tenancies around the corner on
Mackelvie Street. RTA Studio director Richard
Naish has made a specialty of inserting new
buildings into the fabric of Auckland's old
inner-city suburbs. He's not afraid of a bit of
ornament, seeing an expressive façade as
one way to make contextual connections in
neighbourhoods that retain heritage buildings
from a more decorative time. On Mackelvie
Street, the little strip of north-facing shops tip
their roofs to the afternoon sun. The treatment
of the shops' white cement-sheet façades
may be inspired by the pressed-tin ceilings
of their Victorian and Edwardian neighbours,
but on a blue-sky day the effect is more
exotic. It's a long way from Mackelvie Street to
Morocco, but the pattern of the perforations
carries just a suggestion of the souk.

All Saints Church

48

284 Ponsonby Road
Richard Toy, 1958

Richard Toy (1911–1995) — or Richard Horton Beauclerc
Toy, to give him his full name — was born in Canada
and spent his early childhood years in England before
he emigrated with his family to New Zealand in 1923.
A graduate of the University of Auckland's School of
Architecture, Toy spent nearly all of his working life
there, where his articulate ideation of New Zealand's
architecture and landscape influenced generations
of students. He practised as well, and was especially
prolific in the 1950s, when he designed a series of
Anglican churches in Auckland. The best-known is
All Saints, a Church of England outpost in traditionally
Catholic territory at the Three Lamps end of Ponsonby
Road. Critics have proffered a bicultural reading of the
church, likening its roof form to those of Auckland's
nineteenth-century timber churches built under the
direction of Anglican Bishop George Augustus Selwyn,
and its porch and forecourt arrangement to the marae
ātea, the open space in front of a wharenui or meeting
house where visitors are welcomed onto a marae and
debates take place. The zig-zag wall on the Ponsonby
Road façade, another Toy trope, gives a bit of a kink
to the church's straightforward rectangular plan.

Ponsonby Post Office

49

Corner of Ponsonby Road and St Marys Road
John Campbell, 1912
Historic Place Category 1

Government Architect John Campbell (1857–1942),
Baroque stylist and post office specialist, did not hold
back on the design of the post office building that
occupies a corner site at the north end of the Ponsonby
ridge. The building, which, after the post office's
de-accessioning drive, now houses a restaurant, is
a commanding presence on a crossroads quarter —
appellation Three Lamps, after a nineteenth-century
landmark lamppost — that's a gateway to the favoured
inner-city suburbs of Ponsonby, St Marys Bay and
Herne Bay. The building puts its best face forward
on its apex façade, which presents a line-up of main
entry, balustraded parapet, pediment framing the
royal coat of arms, and clock tower. The clock tower
was added a year after the building was completed
and, by popular demand, was 10 feet higher than
originally intended, an augmentation that may be a
factor in the much-loved building's rather awkward
demeanour. In 1920 the Ponsonby Post Office
achieved notoriety when a robber who had murdered
the postmaster for the strongroom keys became
the first person in New Zealand to be convicted on
fingerprint evidence. He was subsequently hanged.

Leys Institute

50

20 St Marys Road
Robert Watt, 1905–1906
Historic Place Category 1

The Leys Institute is a monument to Victorian/Edwardian
philanthropy and philosophies of self-improvement
that, for well over a century, has been a valuable
community asset. The Institute was originally funded by
the bequest of the civic-minded Auckland bookbinder
William Leys (c1850–1899), who wished to coax local
youth out of their layabout tendencies; his wealthier
brother Thomson instigated the construction in 1905,
on Council-donated land, of the Leys Institute Public
Library, and a year later, of the neighbouring gymnasium.
The buildings were designed in the default neo-Baroque
style of contemporary institutional architecture by
Scottish immigrant Robert Martin Watt (1860–1907),
who from the early 1890s was in practice with John
Mitchell (c1859–1947). The Library, which is built of
brick and faced with a cement render, has received
several additions, including a 1958 children's library by
Gummer & Ford; it remains the most graceful element
of an impressive cluster of Edwardian buildings that
includes the old Ponsonby Post Office and, across
the road, next to a restful pocket park, the former
Ponsonby Fire Station (Goldsbro' & Wade, 1902).

A NOTE ABOUT
ARCHITECTURAL STYLES

Nineteenth-century architecture was an architecture of revivalisms. The dominant styles of the Western canon of the previous two millennia were replicated, resuscitated or reinterpreted in relatively quick succession. There was a Classical revival, a Gothic revival and a Baroque revival, to name just the principal architectural re-visitations. Even Arts and Crafts, consciously a departure from the contemporary tendency to stylistic regurgitation, itself harked back to the medieval era of hand-making. These styles, which originated in Europe, became the architectural styles of Europe's empires; in their British iterations, they were successively realised and then overlapped on the streets of the colonial city of Auckland.

Into the twentieth century, the various versions of architectural modernity were duly expressed in the city. Spanish Mission, Art Deco, Moderne and Stripped Classical styles all had their local moment, often executed by architects equipped with a Beaux-Arts awareness of historical architectural styles and design principles. The cautious treatment of Modernism persisted until after the Second World War, when the International Style arrived to take its place as the architecture of the new corporate order.

Art Deco: An architectural and design style fashionable in the 1920s and 1930s that took its name from the influential Exposition Internationale des Arts Décoratifs et Industriels Modernes held in Paris in 1925; a less confrontational Modernism that combined an admiration for machine-age technology with a taste for geometric ornamentation and stylised motifs. A sleeker variant of the style, Moderne or Streamline Moderne, emerged in the 1930s.

Arts and Crafts: The precursor to Modernism, Arts and Crafts architecture evoked the organic nature and functional simplicity of pre-Industrial Age architecture; a movement before it was a style, Arts and Crafts, as its title suggests, prized handcrafted construction and the 'honest' use of natural materials.

Baroque Revival: The architectural style, also called neo- Baroque, of the late nineteenth century inspired by, in Europe, the exuberant Counter-Reformation Baroque style of the sixteenth and seventeenth centuries, and in England by the more Classical architecture of Christopher Wren (1632–1723). At the turn of the twentieth century in Britain and its colonies the style evolved into Edwardian Baroque, the architectural language of late British imperialism, expressed in hefty and august buildings much adorned with ornamental elements.

Beaux-Arts: The rich Classical architectural style taught and promoted by the influential École des Beaux-Arts in Paris from the later nineteenth century until the Second World War.

Chicago School: The term applied to the steel-framed skyscraper architecture pioneered in Chicago in the later nineteenth and early twentieth centuries, and to its practitioners, among them Daniel Burnham and Louis Sullivan.

Classicism (also neo-Classicism): The revival of, or reference to, the principles and forms of Greek or Roman architecture of classical antiquity. A symmetrical and serious architecture of pedestals, columns and pediments, with restrained decoration.

Gothic Revival (also neo-Gothic or Victorian Gothic): The late eighteenth- and nineteenth-century revival, associated with High Church Anglicanism and Roman Catholicism, of the Gothic architecture dominant in England from the twelfth through the fifteenth centuries. In contrast to architecture of the Classical tradition, Gothic (and therefore Gothic Revival) architecture was an architecture of pointy bits — spires, flying buttresses, rib vaults and lancet windows.

French Renaissance (also French Château): A style in vogue in the late nineteenth century that referred to the aristocratic houses (châteaux) of the fifteenth to seventeenth centuries in the Loire Valley; components of the French Renaissance style included towers, spires and steeply pitched roofs, arranged in asymmetric composition. A Beaux-Arts training was useful in realising this style.

International Style: The Modernist architectural style that emerged in Europe after the First World War and spread throughout the world, retaining its dominance until the late 1970s. Characteristics of the style included an emphasis on volume over mass (in contrast to Baroque Revival architecture, for example), the use of lightweight industrial materials, modular forms, flat surfaces and large areas of glazing, and the rejection of ornament.

Italianate: The mid-nineteenth-century tributary of neo-Classical architecture featuring a rectangular building form with gently pitched roofs and overhanging eaves, and deploying a range of Classical details such as corbels, quoins and decorative mouldings. In New Zealand, these traditionally masonry elements were often rendered in timber.

Moderne: Also called Streamline Moderne, this late architectural iteration of Art Deco emerged in the late 1930s. It featured curving forms and horizontal lines and, sometimes, ship-like styling and nautical elements.

Queen Anne Revival: The late nineteenth- and early twentieth-century style that referred, rather loosely, to the Dutch-inflected English Baroque style favoured in the reign of Queen Anne (1702–1714). In its revived form the style was typified by the use of a shallow-pitched roof, turrets, fine brickwork and bands of masonry, and sash windows.

Spanish Mission (or Mission Revival): A style popular in the years before and immediately after the First World War, inspired by late eighteenth- and early nineteenth-century Spanish mission buildings in California. Thick masonry walls, often of white-painted stucco, low-pitched roofs with terracotta tiles and wide eaves, arches and limited glazing characterised the style.

Stripped Classical: Classicism stripped of much if not all ornamentation; an architectural style popular with governments of all types in the inter-war years. The style suggested authority, but it was also a compromise with Modernism, which was becoming the dominant international movement. The Stripped Classical style also had the advantage of economy, as it eschewed the expensive detailing that typified styles such as Baroque Revival and Edwardian Baroque.

GLOSSARY OF ARCHITECTURAL TERMS

Baptistery: The part of a church used for baptisms.

Barrel vault: Semi-circular or cylindrical vault.

Bas-relief: Shallow or low-relief sculptural image projecting from a wall.

Broach spire: A tall, triangular-faced pyramidal or conical spire that sits upon a church tower or turret.

Buttress: Masonry or brickwork projecting from, or built against, a wall to provide structural strength.

Cartouch: Ornamental detail usually sculpted in the form of a scroll or sheet of paper with curling edges.

Chancel: The part of the church around the altar, generally reserved for the clergy and choir.

Console: Ornamental curved bracket, often moulded or sculpted, applied to a wall of a building.

Corbel: Projecting block, usually of stone, supporting a horizontal structural element.

Cupola: Small dome crowning a roof or turret.

Entablature: In Classical architecture, a horizontal superstructure of mouldings and bands that sits above columns.

Frieze: Wide central section of an entablature, often decorated with a bas-relief.

Keystone: Central stone of an arch.

Lancet window: A slender, pointed arch window typical of early Gothic churches of the twelfth and thirteenth centuries.

Mansard roof: Roof with a double slope, the lower being longer and steeper than the upper.

Mullion: Vertical element that divides a window into two or more sections.

Nave: The central part of a church building, usually accommodating the congregation.

Pedestal: In Classical architecture, the base supporting a column.

Pediment: Gable, usually triangular, placed about the horizontal entablature of Classical and Baroque buildings.

Pilaster: Shallow rectangular column projecting from a wall.

Pilotis: French term for pillars that support a building above an open ground floor.

Portico: Roofed space that, open or partly enclosed, leads to the entrance of a building.

Quoins: Dressed stones at the corner of a building.

Sacristy: Room in a church where clerical vestments and sacred objects are kept.

Sanctuary: Area around the main altar in a church.

Spandrel: The triangular space between two arches or between an arch and its rectangular surround.

CONNECTIONS

Architecture is a global pursuit and, like architects everywhere, practitioners in Auckland have always been aware of — at the very least — the work of architects elsewhere. Some of these influential architects are mentioned in this book; they were British at first, naturally, but then the local gaze started to turn to the United States. Tastes became more cosmopolitan as Modernism became the reigning international movement.

Alvar Aalto (1898–1976) was one of the outstanding figures in twentieth-century architecture, much admired for his humanistic application of Modernist design principles; the Finnish architect designed more than 300 buildings, and, in many cases, all their furniture and fittings as well.

Daniel Burnham (1846–1912) was a pioneer of American skyscraper architecture whose work can still be seen in Chicago and other US cities (the Flatiron Building in New York is one of his most famous buildings); his ambition as an urban planner is captured in his dictum, 'Make no small plans'.

Walter Burley Griffin (1876–1937) trained as an architect and landscape architect and worked in Chicago for Frank Lloyd Wright before he and his wife, architect Marion Mahony (1871–1961), won the competition to design Australia's new federal capital of Canberra.

Gertrude Jekyll (1843–1932) was an English plantswoman and garden designer; famed for her colourful and informal planning schemes, she designed more than 400 gardens, many of them for country houses designed by Sir Edwin Lutyens, with whom she worked in close collaboration.

Le Corbusier (1887–1965), born Charles-Édouard Jeanneret, was probably the most famous architect of the twentieth century; the Swiss-born designer, polemicist and urban planner was the author of such canonic Modernist works as the Villa Savoye near Paris, Nôtre Dame-du-Haut at Ronchamps, and the city of Chandigarh in northern India.

Adolf Loos (1870–1933) spent most of his career in Vienna, a city not short of the sort of ornamental architecture to which, as a Modernist theorist, he took exception; in his own architecture he practised what he preached — Emperor Franz Joseph so disliked one of Loos's buildings that he avoided leaving his palace through a gate in its vicinity.

Sir Edwin Lutyens (1869–1944) was widely hailed in his lifetime as the greatest British architect of his age; in his early career he designed numerous country houses in the Arts and Crafts style, but later was inclined to Classicism, which he pursued in the design of acclaimed First World War memorials and imperial buildings in New Delhi.

Ludwig Mies van der Rohe (1886–1969) was the master of large-scale Modernism. Born in Germany, he designed the seminal Barcelona Pavilion and taught at the Bauhaus before moving, in the late 1930s, to America, where he produced such Modernist icons as the Farnsworth House near Chicago and the Seagram Building in New York City.

Pier Luigi Nervi (1891–1979), a renowned Italian structural engineer and maestro of reinforced concrete, worked closely with architects on the design of office towers, stadiums, churches and bridges; his international projects included Sydney's MLC Centre and Australia Square Tower, in collaboration with Harry Seidler.

Richard Neutra (1892–1970) was an Austrian-born architect of Jewish descent who practised in Berlin before migrating to America in the 1920s; there he became a foremost exponent of the crisp, cool, open-plan architecture that typified mid-century Californian Modernism.

Gio Ponti (1891–1979) was a Milanese architect, designer and publisher; he undertook significant commercial and institutional projects before and during the Second World War, and as an omni-talented designer and editor of the influential design magazine *Domus* became one of the faces of the post-war Italian *miracolo econimico*.

Augustus Pugin (1812–1852), architect, critic, Catholic convert and leading figure in the English nineteenth-century revival of Gothic or 'pointed' architecture, is best known for designing the interior of the Palace of Westminster (the Houses of Parliament); he also designed numerous churches in England, Ireland and Australia.

Sir George Gilbert Scott (1811–1878) was a prominent and prolific English Gothic Revival architect; he designed scores of churches and cathedrals, including ChristChurch Cathedral (destroyed in the 2011 Christchurch earthquake), as well as workhouses, lunatic asylums, schools and the Albert Memorial in London.

Harry Seidler (1923–2006) is the giant of Australian Modernism; born in Austria and educated at Harvard, he worked for Marcel Breuer in New York and Oscar Niemeyer in Brazil before he migrated to Sydney with his family, designed a famous house for his mother — the Rose Seidler House — and then practised flamboyantly for almost 60 years.

Skidmore, Owings & Merrill (SOM), an American architectural practice established in the 1930s, became the leading international exponent of corporate high-rise Modernism; its founders were derided by Frank Lloyd Wright as the 'three blind Mies' but SOM has designed such acclaimed skyscrapers as Lever House (New York, 1952) and the Sears Tower (Chicago, 1973) and, more latterly, the world's tallest building, the Burj Khalifa in Dubai.

Louis Sullivan (1856–1924) is synonymous with the advent of the steel-framed skyscraper and the rise of Chicago as a great architectural centre; although the Modernist mantra 'form follows function' is attributed to Sullivan, he was celebrated for the skilful application of ornamental detail to his elegant buildings.

FURTHER READING

Much information on Auckland's architecture and architects is contained in Peter Shaw's *A History of New Zealand Architecture*. The third edition of the book (Hodder Moa Beckett, 2003) is the most useful and remains the standard survey of the subject.

John Stacpoole (1919–2018), a pioneering historian of the colonial period of New Zealand architecture, wrote about early Auckland architecture in Architecture 1820–1970 (A. H. & A. W. Reed, 1972), a book co-authored by architect Peter Beaven, and in Colonial Architecture in New Zealand (A. H. & A. W. Reed, 1976).

For a more complete understanding of New Zealand's architectural history, works on colonial-era architecture may be complemented by Deirdre Brown's Māori Architecture: From Fale to Wharenui and Beyond (Penguin, 2009).

Julia Gatley, who teaches at the School of Architecture and Planning at the University of Auckland, has covered twentieth-century Auckland architecture in Long Live the Modern: New Zealand's New Architecture, 1904–1984 (Auckland University Press, 2008), and Group Architects: Towards a New Zealand Architecture (Auckland University Press, 2010).

Errol Haarhoff's Guide to the Architecture of Central Auckland (Balasoglou Books, 2006) profiles 100 buildings located in Auckland's CBD and inner suburbs.

Block, the publishing arm of the Auckland branch of the New Zealand Institute of Architects, has put out a series of more than 50 architecture guides since 2006; more than half are dedicated to aspects of Auckland architecture and the work of Auckland-based practices. The Block guides may be viewed and downloaded at http://www.architecture-archive.auckland.ac.nz.

Award-winning Auckland buildings from the past decade are presented on the website of the New Zealand Institute of Architects: www.nzia.co.nz.

ACKNOWLEDGEMENTS

The authors thank Auckland Live for permission to photograph the interior of the Civic Theatre, the administrator of the Maclaurin Chapel for permission to photograph the interior of the chapel, and, above all, Catherine Hammond for her invaluable assistance.

INDEX

First published in 2019 by Massey University Press
Private Bag 102904, North Shore Mail Centre
Auckland 0745, New Zealand
www.masseypress.ac.nz

In association with the New Zealand Institute of Architects

Text copyright © John Walsh, 2019
Images copyright © Patrick Reynolds, 2019
Design by The Letter Q

Printed and bound in China

ISBN: 978-0-9951135-3-4

With the support of The Warren Trust and APL

THE WARREN TRUST